The Gift of the Dragonfly

The Gift of the Dragonfly

poems of transformation
Kelly Sollinger

Scripture quotations marked NIV are taken from the Holy Bible, New International Version®, NIV®. Copyright © 1973, 1978, 1984, 2011 by Biblica, Inc.™ Used by permission of Zondervan. All rights reserved worldwide. www.zondervan.com The "NIV" and "New International Version" are trademarks registered in the United States Patent and Trademark Office by Biblica, Inc.™

Scripture texts marked NAB are taken from the *New American Bible, revised edition* © 2010, 1991, 1986, 1970 Confraternity of Christian Doctrine, Washington, D.C. and are used by permission of the copyright owner. All Rights Reserved. No part of the New American Bible may be reproduced in any form without permission in writing from the copyright owner.

Scripture quotations marked ESV are from are from The ESV® Bible (The Holy Bible, English Standard Version®), © 2001 by Crossway, a publishing ministry of Good News Publishers. Used by permission. All rights reserved.

Scripture quotations marked MSG are taken from *The Message*, copyright © 1993, 2002, 2018 by Eugene H. Peterson. Used by permission of NavPress. All rights reserved. Represented by Tyndale House Publishers.

Dragonfly larvae and hatching photos by Illuvis and Criadero via Pixabay.
Dragonfly photo by Garvit Nama on Unsplash.

© 2024 by Kelly Sollinger, Dancing Owl Press

All rights reserved. No part of this book may be reproduced, or stored in a retrieval system, or transmitted in any form or by any means, electronic, mechanical, photocopying, recording, or otherwise, without express written permission of the publisher.

Permission is granted for one-time reproduction of individual poems for worship and spiritual direction purposes, provided that the following credit line is included:
© Kelly Sollinger from *The Gift of the Dragonfly: Poems of Transformation*, dancingowlstudio.com

Paperback: ISBN - 979-8-9904021-0-2

To all the strong women who formed me and continue to support me on this path:

Mom, who always believed in me even when she didn't understand me or my calling.

Tonja, who has always gently nudged me into finding my voice.

Barbara, who gave me the language to articulate the jumble of thoughts.

Liz, who helped me see my true callings.

Contents

Dragonflies 2
Who is God?
      visiting god   8
      the god who is coming   9
      a message   10
      i am not asking you   11
      jesus whispered   12
      getting lost   13
      gentle, patient jesus   14
      loving god   16
      the god of my childhood   18
Suffering and Brokenness
      suffering's alchemy   24
      sighing   25
      broken   26
      in the garden   28
Trust
      trust me   34
      i believe   35
      trusting you   36
      litany of trust   37
      what do you do   38
      there is a space   39
      listen to my song   40

Waiting
- speed   46
- feast   47
- blessed are those   48
- waiting   50
- what we see   51
- exhale... inhale…   52
- a prayer for the in-between time   53
- inhale... exhale…   54
- your voice   55

Transformation
- like a baby   60
- enough   61
- my heart   62
- unburdened   64
- lost   66
- to the idol   68
- the gift of the dragonfly   70

New Life
- we clutch at the past   76
- just the beginning   77
- god of the journey   78
- without me   79
- what is love   80
- blessed am i   82
- my unique service   83
- abundance   84
- silence   85

Epilogue
- how does one write a poem?   89

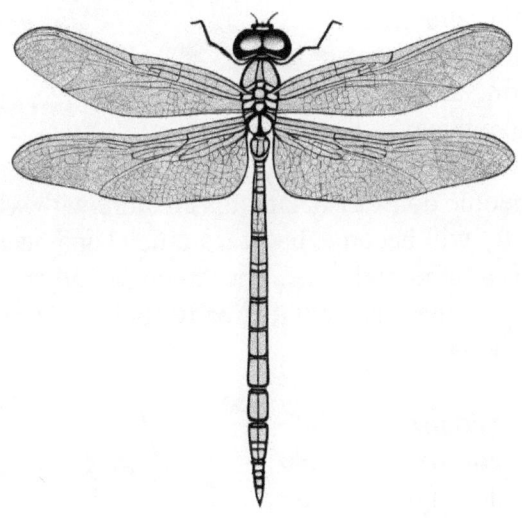

Dragonflies

To appreciate this book, it will help to know a bit about the life cycle of a dragonfly. This wasn't how you expected a book of poetry to begin, but please bear with me.

A dragonfly hatches from an egg and then spends much of its life as a rather drab-looking larva, living underwater and eating all the time. They live this way for months or even years.

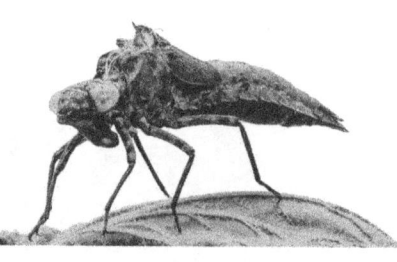

Most people don't associate this creature with what the dragonfly will become, but it's a crucial and necessary stage, if a rather ugly one. The "pond-bound creature" is called a "nymph," and it already contains all that it will someday be.

Over the course of their life, dragonflies will molt several dozen times. Old skin sheds to make way for new skin. On the last molting, they climb out of their insect shell sporting wings and the ability to breathe air. They are transformed, but the process happened over a lifetime.

When we think of transformation, we might call to mind a butterfly: a worm crawls into a cocoon and comes out something completely different. I think a dragonfly is closer to what actually happens to us over the course of our lives. We are born with talents and gifts. Some of those become evident early on. Many take decades to fully develop and blossom. Moments of transformation are like the dragonfly stepping out of the last old skin: we are completely new, but everything was already there from the start.

For most of us, it takes a lifetime of shedding the unnecessary to uncover the essence of who we are. This is the process of transformation: learning who our creator is, enduring times of suffering, trusting, waiting, and eventually coming into new life.

The gift of the dragonfly is knowing that the process has a purpose and is leading us towards something far better than we could ever imagine.

I kneel before the Father, from whom every family in heaven and on earth derives its name. I pray that out of his glorious riches he may strengthen you with power through his Spirit in your inner being, so that Christ may dwell in your hearts through faith. And I pray that you, being rooted and established in love, may have power, together with all the Lord's holy people, to grasp how wide and long and high and deep is the love of Christ, and to know this love that surpasses knowledge—that you may be filled to the measure of all the fullness of God. Now to him who is able to do immeasurably more than all we ask or imagine, according to his power that is at work within us, to him be glory in the church and in Christ Jesus throughout all generations, for ever and ever! Amen.

Ephesians 3 NIV

Who is God?

I grew up with a very stern and remote God. I often call him my "index card God." This God, in my imagination, had an index card on which was written the plan of my life. To be sure, none of the things on that card were things I was good at, much less particularly enjoyed. My job was to figure out what was on the card so that God would be happy and I could, maybe, be happy too. The trick was that God would not show me the card. At best, he might give hints, but I was on my own to figure it out. I lived in fear that I was doing everything wrong.

The starting point for all spiritual journeys is a person's image of God. If you imagine a deity who does not communicate, judges harshly, keeps score, and is just waiting for an opportunity to punish, your approach to such a being will most likely be cautious and closed. At least that was true for me. It took years of work to expose false images and make room for who God wanted to reveal herself to be.

Is God male or female? I grew up with a very male image of God. Certainly, the Holy Spirit could be called "she," but God—a Father, a man. No question about it.

Along the way of my journey, God has constantly pushed the boundaries I set for who God is, including the boundary of gender. I've come to know the first person of the Trinity as decidedly feminine. This has allowed me to see in God the best qualities of all the strong women I've been blessed to know.
One of these poems came out of trying to share my image of God with someone. Trying to describe an indescribable God is no small task! But, for me, it might start as a conversation over tea on a comfortable couch.

There have been times in the last few years of my spiritual journey when I wanted very much to move forward. I could see that God was inviting me to progress in experiencing her, but I was too afraid of what that might mean. Never once did God force or push me. Looking back, I see the patient work of God. I see each time I took even a hesitant step forward, it was as though God cheered me on, celebrating even a tiny bit of faith in action. Even the times I was paralyzed by fear, God remained patiently waiting, never forcing, ever gentle.

For a very long time I thought I was looking for God. I felt a need for God's presence that I could not explain to myself, let alone anyone else. I sought God everywhere in everything, praying that she would make herself known. It took me a long time to accept the seemingly simple fact that God is always present, always near.

The God I know today is lavish and abundant in loving. I have come to know God as not only feminine but quite gentle. This God constantly sends messages of her love in so many ways. This God desires me infinitely more than I could ever desire her and, yet, somehow, my desire for her mirrors her desire for me. I am constantly reminded that God cannot *not* love us.

I desire to draw closer and closer to this God I have come to know. At times I'm tempted to think perhaps God does not understand this longing within me to know her more deeply. And then there are moments when I know I can't begin to understand this longing within God to know me more deeply.

visiting god

once i went to visit god
walked right up the sidewalk
knocked on her door
she answered as though
she'd been standing there
      watching for me
      all day
she flung open the door
embraced me in a hug
then stepped back
and gestured to
the couch
      god never says a whole lot
      in my experience
           but just you watch
she brought my favorite tea
      she knows me well like that
and then sat down
head cocked and looked at me
when god looks at me like that
i just want to sit here
      let the tea get cold
      and look back
what else can you do
in god's living room
when god smiles at you

the god who is coming

"We cannot talk God into coming by longer and more urgent prayer. We simply need to open to God's ever-present coming."
Fr. Vinny McKiernan, C.S.P.

the god who is coming
is the god
who already came

the god who already came
is the god who comes
moment by moment

the god who comes
moment by moment
is the god
always present

this is a great mystery
never fully explained
only lived into
breath by breath

a message

i am at the pond
seeking something
i cannot name
needing to feel
god near

a flock of ducks
ranges about
in the grass
one brave soul
breaks from the group
a prophet
dressed in green
waddling past
with a message
      god says
       i love you
        don't forget
leaving me to ponder
the many ways
christ speaks

i am not asking you

i am not asking you
to go to timbuktu
i am not saying
you must do impossible things
i am not sending you
to cross an ocean
climb a mountain
or trek the desert

i am simply
giving
and giving
and giving
i am just
waiting
for you
to receive

jesus whispered

jesus whispered
      i love you
like a lover
telling his beloved
a secret
the whole world knows
but it feels like a delicious
delight
meant only for my ears
      i love you

getting lost

sometimes I get lost
in the art of creation
making things that weren't
there before

is that how you feel
when I sit in the silent darkness
waging war with darting thoughts
sometimes feeling alone
yet always
always
in your presence

what are you creating
in the depths of me?
do you get lost sometimes
with the sheer delight of it?
when will I see
the cover pulled back
the canvas revealed?
what will I be?
will I find you there?

gentle, patient jesus

gentle jesus
always meeting me
where i am
inviting
wooing
consoling
but never forcing
never pushing me
where i am afraid
to go

patient jesus
preparing my heart
little by little
day by day
transforming me
one breath
at a time

loving god

loving god

for all the lies
we accept
      we are not good enough
      smart enough
      pretty enough
      clever enough
and that biggest lie of all
      we are not loved
forgive us

for all the times
we choose
      to rely on ourselves
      to trust in what we can do
      to believe we do not need you
forgive us

forgive us for trying
to measure up
to a god whose love
for us
is immeasurable
remind us again and again
of the
ineffable
outrageousness
of that love made flesh
for love of us

let us see ourselves
as you see us
        a priceless treasure
        a delight
        loved beyond telling

give us the grace
to love ourselves
at least
half as much
as you love us
loving god

the god of my childhood

the god of my childhood
kept score of my sins
    that god
    demanded payment in full
    before any goods
    were given
the god of my childhood
was stern and aloof
    that god
    held up a finger
    shook his head
    and said no no no
    that god
    was eternally disappointed in me
the god of my childhood
was not always around
    that god
    surely had
    more important business
    than the likes of me

i have looked and looked
for the god of my childhood
but that god
    is nowhere to be found

the god of my maturity
is too busy
        lavishing good things on me
        giving all i desire
        and then some
the god of my maturity
has open arms
        to embrace
        and welcome all
        of who i am
the god of my maturity
is never not present
        always here
        loving me into existence

the god of my maturity
has taught me
that the god of my childhood
        was a god
        of my own making

Suffering and Brokenness

The human condition constantly forces us to confront brokenness in all its many forms—our own and that of others. Ancient wisdom teaches that brokenness and the suffering that results are, paradoxically, gateways to transformation.

The role of suffering in spiritual transformation seems out of place at first glance. It's something we're wired to avoid. Jesus never asks us to embrace suffering in and of itself. At the same time, we know that suffering is an inevitable part of growth. Medieval alchemists sought to turn base metals into gold. The tears of suffering work to produce something far more valuable.

Even Jesus asked the Father to be able to bypass his suffering. I always find strength in this very human request. It is natural to want to avoid the pain. And yet, Jesus shows us it is only through pain that we can embrace the resurrected life. How did he do it? Love.

suffering's alchemy

how can this be
that your presence
is magnified
in the pain—
so that it is
pain
which transforms
into pure love?

like john before me
I bear witness
to the light
      a light magnified
      through suffering

suffering's alchemy—
turning tears
into
golden joy

sighing

"All my longings lie open before you, Lord; my sighing is not hidden from you."
Psalm 38:9 NIV

lord you know
the cares of my heart
hear my sighs
inhabit them
so that all
is you

broken

"They all ate and were satisfied. And what was left over was picked up, twelve baskets of broken pieces."
Luke 9:17 ESV

the sun glimmers on the pieces
hope in the midst of despair
broken pieces
a new picture emerges
not what once was
or could be
      can never be again
but something new
mended
patched
repaired
into something wholly unexpected

unexpectedly holy

nothing is all bad
nothing is all good
a broken mix
a mixed brokenness

i will not give in to despair
no matter how many pieces
lie around me
i am made whole
made anew
fashioned out of
      broken pieces

bread unbroken
cannot be shared
cannot be received
broken and multiplied
given to all in pieces
for a greater good
not one piece is lost

i am blessed
and beautifully broken

in the garden

"If it is possible, may this cup be taken from me."
Matthew 26:39 NIV

in the garden we pray
over all the impossibilities—
can we avoid suffering?
can we escape pain?
could there be a way other than
        death
to get to
        resurrection?
we wrestle with the questions
        again
        and again
        and again

must i?

can i?

will i?

i like to imagine
you thought of your mother
there in the garden
        how she said yes
        against all odds—
        how love makes us do
        impossible things

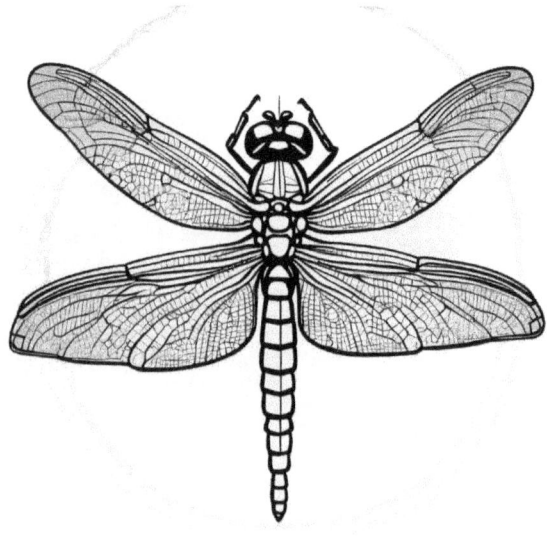

# Trust

According to the dictionary, trust is "a firm belief in the reliability, truth, ability, or strength of someone or something." I don't know about you, but trust does not come easily to me, and I do not give it lightly to anyone.

It took me a long time to start trusting God. Even now it is sometimes a daily work in progress. Some days I can firmly believe that God is reliable, but I do not act as though God is strong enough. Or I may believe God is able but not willing. With each breath, I must choose trust in God.

One poem about trust came during a retreat when I felt God inviting me into a deeper trust. It was like being in an oar-less boat with absolutely no control over anything. At the same time, I knew I was in Christ, who has control over absolutely everything. It's a tension of trust.

I find journaling extremely valuable because it helps me take a longer view. I recall a day I was journaling during an unsettled season. I was busy with ministry work that I enjoyed, but I was tired, and prayer felt dry, desolate, and frustrating. A phrase from my reading that Advent morning jumped out at me: "God unseen is taking form." I desperately wanted to believe it. I wanted to trust that God was working in some way I could not yet see, could not even begin to imagine. Over the course of several days, I continued to ponder this in my journal. The more I reflected and wrote, the deeper my trust became. God, unseen, was indeed taking form, and my trust grew stronger by the day. Developing trust takes time.

I once made a piece of art in a little notebook with John 16:24 "ask and you shall receive." On one page I wrote the word *ask* and on the opposite page I wrote *receive*. It hit me with such clarity: there is a space between that asking and receiving. Prayers are rarely ever answered immediately. What happens in that space is what happens in all such liminal spaces: transformation. And trust is the bridge that gets us through it.

There have been times in life when I thought I was not trusting. And yet, I look back and realize that if God had not been there, I would have been overwhelmed and defeated. Perhaps I didn't know in the moment that I was trusting God, but I was. Trust is sometimes only apparent in hindsight.

trust me

come into the boat
but leave your paddle
on the shore
                            trust me

i know where we're going
and i know how to go there
                            trust me

when the waves toss us about
hold on to the boat
hold on to me
              same thing
                            trust me

where are we going?
how will we get there?
how will we know we're there?
                            trust me

my yoke is easy
my burden light
the hardest thing
is putting yours down
              your yokes
              your burdens
                            trust me

i am the boat
i am the oar
i am the way, the truth, the life
i am all you long for
your deepest desire
                            trust me

i believe

i believe
from the soles of my feet
to the crown of my head
into the depths of my heart
i believe
you are working
in and through me
      every moment
      each circumstance
to bring about more good
than i could ever imagine
possible
i believe

trusting you

jesus
help me trust you
I want to trust you
I do trust you
bless all the
spaces within me
that are not yet ready
to trust
bless all the
places in me
that are just beginning
to trust
bless all the
graces in me
that are taking root
in the soil of your trust
in me
help me grow
more deeply into
trusting you

litany of trust

"I know what I'm doing. I have it all planned out—plans to take care of you, not abandon you, plans to give you the future you hope for. When you call on me, when you come and pray to me, I'll listen."
Jeremiah 29:11-12 MSG

that you know what you are doing
> jesus i trust you

that you have it all planned out
> jesus i trust you

that you have holy plans for me
> jesus i trust you

that you have plans to care for me
> jesus i trust you

that you have plans to give me
the future i hope for
> jesus i trust you

that you always hear me
> jesus i trust you

that you can always be found
> jesus i trust you

that your love for me is eternal
> jesus i trust you

what do you do

what do you do
when god has gone
off to tend
some important business
what do you do
when the will to pray
has dried up
and blown away
what do you do
when you're in the boat
all alone
drifting aimlessly
what do you do
when god seems gone
and you feel lost

when my kids were little
and we would go out
i would tell them
   if you get lost
   stop
   sit down
   don't move
   i will find you
   but you must be still

is that my task today god?
   stop
   sit down
   be still
   know myself already found

there is a space

"Ask and you will receive."
John 16:24 NIV

there is a space
between ask
and receive
a place for god to work
transforming what i ask
into what i need

when i don't know
what to ask
no matter!
god does the asking
in and for
and through me
making prayer
out of it all

listen to my song

Psalm 124

if the lord had not been on my side
    listen to my song
if the lord had not been on my side
when the trials of life
rose up against me
their angry rage
would have devoured me
    swallowed me whole
their storms would have
    swept me away

blessed be the lord my god
who has cradled me
    safe
like a butterfly
    i have escaped from the net
    to fly free
even the times i was caught
god broke the net
so i could escape

my help is in the lord
who made heaven and earth
listen to my song

Waiting

What is any journey without times of waiting? The journey towards knowing our God more intimately necessarily means waiting for God to move in us, as well as the space and silence to notice those movements. Waiting can be challenging and taxing, and yet, it is precisely those times of waiting that shape us into people who can wait on the Lord.

There are times in our life when God has filled us to the brim with goodness. Soon we will begin to share that goodness with others, but this particular moment is a chance to wait, savor God's grace, and let it change us.

There are other times in the journey when we have worked for God and worked hard. We are exhausted and depleted. It is almost time to rest. Whether we observe it or not, there is always a space, a pause between the activity and the resting. A time to slow down and make room for grace to begin her work.

speed

when i move
at the speed
of the world
  it's all a blur
when i stop
and listen
i taste you
  so very near
help me to move
at the speed of grace

feast

despair may abound
but i will not
feast on it
you become
what you consume
therefore
i will eat
the meager ration
of joy today
        a cat's purr
        a sip of hot tea
        the quiet dawn
these alone will i consume
these will i enjoy
in the patient
waiting
for them to grow into you
feast beyond all telling

blessed are those

You that fear the Lord, wait for his mercy,
   do not stray lest you fall.
You that fear the Lord, trust in him,
   and your reward will not be lost.
You that fear the Lord, hope for good things,
   for lasting joy and mercy.
Sirach 2:7-9 NAB

blessed are those
who wait
>   not with impatient
>   tapping of foot
>   wanting to be elsewhere

blessed are those
who wait
in joyful expectation
of what is to come
cultivating the soil
all the while

blessed are those
who trust
>   not trust-with-a-backup-plan-B
>   expecting failure
>   at every turn

blessed are those
who trust
in god so fully
that every breath
is an affirmation
of complete
and utter dependence

blessed are those
who hope
        not a care-less hope
        without expectation
        of what might be
blessed are those
whose hope
is so strong
it builds a bridge
into the future
spanning doubt and fear
hope so alive
it brings into being
the love waited on
trusted in
longed for

waiting

wait
      you whisper
for what
      i plead
wait
      is your reply

and so i wait
for what i do not know
but for what i know
is coming

wait

what we see

we do not see
all that you
are doing
but the joyful
anticipation
deepens
as we see
what we can
and hope for
what we cannot

exhale... inhale...

this is the space
between the exhale
and the inhale
between letting go
and finding new life
between releasing
and receiving

a silent space
where nothing happens

a silent space
where everything happens

a prayer for the in-between time

bless this in-between time
   transition
   liminal space
one thing fully ripened
another just conceived

in this time
   they meet

may the fruitfulness
of what i have done
enliven
what is to come

may the promise
of what is to come
enlighten
what i have done

in shadow and darkness
   hidden from view
grant me patience
for all the growth
i cannot yet see

grant me vision
for all that is
coming to life in me

inhale... exhale...

this is the space
between the inhale
and the exhale
a nourishing time
of fullness
holding all the goodness
close to my heart
so much grace received
held
in time suspended
this is the space
between taking in
and letting go
holding all that is good
changing it somehow
being changed by it
grace upon grace

your voice

your voice
whispering still
and small
in my heart
        i love you
        i am with you
        you are mine
        i love you
in my heart
a small
still whispering
your voice

Transformation

The ultimate goal of our life is to live with God forever, a state that begins right here and now. But first we must be moved from our narrow blindness into the expansive light of the God who loves us. A transformation is required, a change that leaves us wholly different and yet brings us into our authentic selves, into all we were created to be.

Transformation is often painful as we are deconstructed and then put together anew. As Jesus put it, unless a grain of wheat falls to the ground and dies, it can never bear fruit. It must be transformed into something new.

like a baby

like a baby
with chubby hands
grasping fingers
uncoordinated
uncontrolled
i reach for you
certain
i can hold you
baffled
to find i cannot
batting the air
in silent frustration
only to find
my hand
grasped firmly
by yours

enough

if today i can be
just a tiny bit
  more
    open
than i was
  yesterday
if today i can be
just a little bit
  more
    loving
than i was
  yesterday
if today i can be
just a tad bit
  more
    free
than i was
  yesterday

that will be enough

my heart

"I will remove from them their heart of stone and give them a heart of flesh."
Ezekiel 11:19 NIV

my heart of stone
closed on itself
fearful
suspicious
overwhelmed by everything
my heart of stone
built walls of solid metal
to keep myself in
and others out
my heart of stone
deflected everything
from praise to rejection
my heart of stone
cried invisible tears
longing to be free
from all that caged it

did you know
god can melt
stone?
did you know
god can open a heart
tightly
impossibly
closed?

did you know
god can breathe life
into what is dead
recreate
what has been
destroyed?

my new heart
beats to the tune
of god's love
is colored with the scent
of that love
through and through
my new heart
is alive
with god's touch
radiates that touch
to any who will listen
my new heart
is held in the palm
of god's hand
open to all god gives
receiving the graces
secure in god's love

my heart of stone
has been made anew
into a living
heart of love

unburdened

"On a Sabbath Jesus was teaching in one of the synagogues, and a woman was there who had been crippled by a spirit for eighteen years. She was bent over and could not straighten up at all."
Luke 13:10-11 NIV

it started as such
a little thing
      a tiny worry
      a twinge of anxiety
i carried it around
easily enough
      thought nothing of it at all
      really
one day though
i realized it had grown
heavier
      not as easy
      to carry around
and yet i could not
would not
put it down

i carried it
day after day
sunrise after sunrise
feeling it grow
with each new dawn
others started to see
my burden
after a while
i did not notice them
my gaze held down
by all i carried

by the time i arrived
in the synagogue that day
eighteen long years
had passed
my burden so heavy
i was bent in two
no sunlight ever reached my face

but he saw me
        me
        not my burden
        me
he saw and said
woman
you are set free
from what has bound you
        won't you leave it here?
with that he reached out
        and touched me
and before i knew
what had happened
i was looking him
straight in the eye

look at me now
and you will see
what it is like to be free
from what has kept you
burdened

lost

i have navigated
these days
to this shore
and now
   i feel lost
i have beached my boat
on squishy sand
cutting rocks
steep grade
while not inviting
better than
where i was
but now
   i feel lost
to turn back
to the little boat
to be at neptune's
wit and whim once more
i do not want
and yet i peer
through the mists
to see—maybe—
what i have missed
out there on the water
   i feel lost
to turn and push forward
onto a terrain unknown
and uninviting
holding only a promise
in my heart
feels like a reckless endeavor
"what if..." resounds
"maybe..." reverberates
"possibly..." threatens
to tear my heart
and all its promise
in two

jagged edges
   i feel lost
"and yet..."
"maybe..."
"possibly..."
turn my gaze
away from what was
to what might be
hope tugs
suggests better things
just over the horizon
pulls me
toward what i cannot
yet see
   being found
   lost in you
it was you
who brought me here
through the storms
in a creaky little boat
it was you
who beached me here
on this barren shore
teeming with life
you are the promise
deep in my heart
urging me on
"what if..."
"maybe..."
"and yet..."
you fill all the questions
with hope
pulling me
deeper and deeper
to realize
the lostness i feel
is really only
the spaciousness of you

to the idol

"Those who cling to worthless idols forfeit the grace that could be theirs."
Jonah 2:8 NIV

to the idol
of certainty i cling
sure of my own ways
and beliefs
trusting them
to take me
to you

to the idol
of trust in myself
I cling
sure that everyone always
fails me somehow
easier not to try

to these
and other
worthless idols i cling
forfeiting the grace
that could be mine
clinging so tightly
to what i know
        what i think i know
my hands are not free
to cling to you

pry open my fingers, lord
and take from me
these worthless idols
let me know
your strong
loving
gentle
embrace
guide my hands
to cling to you
to grasp the grace
that is mine
    always and forever
    you

the gift of the dragonfly

the gift of the dragonfly
is not
its iridescent wings
sparkling in the morning sun

the gift of the dragonfly
is not
the arc it traces
from pond to stalk
and back again

the gift of the dragonfly
is not
its long sleek body
trailing like a kite tail
in the breeze

the gift of the dragonfly
is in
the pond-bound creature
shedding layer after layer
always itself
yet ever losing
that which is no longer
necessary
until the day
wings appear
and the water-dweller becomes
everything
she ever dreamed possible

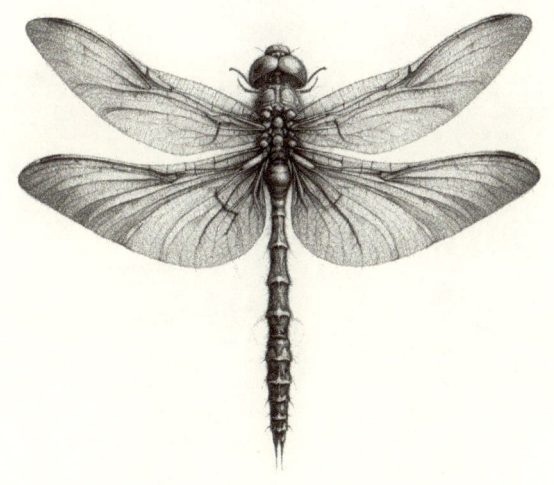

New Life

Life is more a circle than a straight line. We can get our image of God set, recognize our brokenness and suffering, patiently trust God through the process, endure tremendous transformations, and come into new life, only to find ourselves back at a new image of God shedding light on a new area of brokenness. And so the cycle continues. We are constantly being transformed into new life.

we clutch at the past

we clutch at the past
        grasp at the familiar
        at what we know
even as we long
        to be made new
grant us the grace o lord
        to open our hearts and hands
        to release
        what is leaving
        and embrace
        all that is coming

just the beginning

"Jesus said to her, 'You are right when you say you have no husband. The fact is, you have had five husbands, and the man you now have is not your husband. What you have just said is quite true.'"
John 4:17-18 NIV

many things are true
but they do not have to be
the end of the story

maybe you've had five husbands
and the one now
is not a husband

maybe this is just the beginning
of a story
where that
does not matter

god of the journey

"The LORD said to Abram: 'Go forth...'"
Genesis 12:1 NAB

god of the journey
you call each one of us
to transformation
you call us to cooperate
with the work you are doing
in us and in the world

in knowing you
in loving you
in being loved by you
we are changed
moment by moment

give us ears
to listen to you
eyes to see ourselves
as you see us
    beloved child of God
    with whom you are well pleased
help us feel the touch
that comforts
strengthens
and transforms us
raise us up
out of our fear
so that we see only you
shining out of every
person
place
and thing
as we journey home
together

without me

without my voice
in the great song
the harmony would be
incomplete

i am nothing
i am everything
i am all that god
envisioned

i am a vital strand
in god's tapestry
a vivid stroke
in god's painting

without me
the world would tilt
to a little less
joy
happiness
beauty

what is love

how patient must i be
  to see the end result—
  7 days?
  7 hours?
  7 lifetimes?
no... seventy times seven
  patience multiplied and taxed
  beyond measure
  and then some
                that is love

how kind must i be
  to those who are anything but—
  to the ones who test my patience
  who stretch it to the limits
    and beyond
  the kindness that gives a cup of water
  to the very hand
  that withheld it from me
  and gives
  and gives
  and patiently gives
                that is love

the "nots" are easier?
   just root out envy, boasting, pride,
   rudeness, self-interest, anger,
   delighting in others' misfortunes
   tear up the list of wrongs
     from today
   try to start fresh tomorrow
                       that is love

in short, be perfect
   as your father in heaven is perfect—
   unfailing, unflagging, unfettered perfection
start with patience and kindness
   to yourself first of all—
   it's a long journey
   to walk in the way of love
   god has a lot of work to do
                       that is love

blessed am i

"Blessed are you who are poor, for yours is the kingdom of God."
Luke 6:20 NIV

bless me lord
for i am poor

i lack wisdom
nobility
strength
sometimes i lack the will
to seek justice
let alone humility

and yet you say
that my blessing
is in my very
poverty
because it is only in
poverty
that i come to depend
on you

blessed am i lord
for i am poor
and have only
you
who are everything

my unique service

Inspired by "A Prayer" by John Henry Cardinal Newman

god has created me
for some particular service
that is uniquely mine
   no one else can do it!
only in the end
joined to god
will i fully see all the good
god will do through me
   a vital part of his holy plan
i am sent to do his work
to preach his love
in my own way

some days it does not seem
like i am doing much
yet i trust
   always trust
the working of his plan
and his love for me

nothing is outside the scope
of his work—
sickness and grief serve
just as much as wellness and joy
everything matters
everything is part
of his holy plan for me

abundance

joy is
that first sip
of hot coffee
burning as it goes down
that first glimpse
of orange sky
the cold blowing in
with the cat
your shimmering presence
reminding me
this is a new day
full of abundant possibilities

silence

so noisy out here
in the early morning

one bird insists
on her love for you
over and over and over
plaintive and longing

while a flock
insists their praise of you
loud and long

a hawk sits silently
surveying all the sound
bearing witness
that silence
has its own things to say

Epilogue

how does one write a poem?

if you asked how i write a poem. . .

i would tell you
that i don't write
these poems
that they are
pure gift
i would tell you
they flow out of my pen
on to the paper
that all i do
is copy them down
i would tell you
i don't know where
the words come from

all this is true

these words are given to me
for you
the gift of expressing
what is inside
is pure gift
freely received
and freely given

Kelly Sollinger is an artist, writer, teacher, and poet. After almost three decades in software engineering, she embraced a life of creative curiosity, leaving the "safe" zone to explore forgotten parts of herself. This is her first collection of poetry. A native Texan, she currently lives in Columbus, Ohio, with her daughter and three cats.

www.ingramcontent.com/pod-product-compliance
Lightning Source LLC
Chambersburg PA
CBHW020947090426
42736CB00010B/1309